Love, Sex,

and

Sorrow

Tigest Beyene

Life Chronicles Publishing
Give your life a voice!

ISBN: 978-1-950649-81-5

Cover: Graphic Design

Editor: Michelle Anderl

Life Chronicles Publishing Copyright © 2021

lifechroniclespublishing.com

TABLE

OF

CONTENTS

Chapter 1
WHY?

I remember waking up to the sound of whispers and sight of white coats around me. I remember trying to figure out what had just happened to me and why. The numb legs from not moving and the stiff arm from the IV. Looking around me and seeing different machines. The people in the white coats still going back and forth with each other and not even noticing that I am awake.

Finally, I spoke and I got someone's attention. They rushed to my side and started to ask me questions like how I was feeling, reassuring me that everything was going to be okay. I pulled myself up from the bed and noticed a patch on my left side covered with blood. Family started to walk in and hold my hand, repeating, "It's going to be okay."

I then turned my head to the doctor, and she said words that I thought I would never hear: "You have been shot twice."

So many things were running through my head, like "Why would this happen to me?"

I guess my life had just gotten started.

Chapter 2

WHO I AM TODAY

"Hurry up, honey! We are going to be late!" I'm trying to get my daughter up for school and heading out in a rush is normal routine every morning. I am so happy that I am a mother and all, but man do I need a break. I have school and work, and I live with my mother who works two jobs herself. I have to balance these with trying to keep the house together.

I can say though my family is hands on, and I am one of the lucky ones.

I am from Seattle, and yes, it does rain, but when the sun shines, it shines bright. Our summers are just beautiful, walking on the strip of Alki Beach or the dock at Coulon Beach, playing in sand, and just sitting back and enjoying the views. Even though it is a big city, it's small in the African community. Everybody seems to be related or what we call "like my cousin." Most of us hang out at the same club or hookah joint.

My family has been here about thirty years. We are from Ethiopia in the beautiful continent of Africa. My parents split up when I was twelve years old, and even though I truly did not understand what was going on, all I wanted was just to be with my dad. At one point I started to act up and my mom was not having it, so I stayed with my dad. I spent a lot of my time at my cousin's house, too. I call her JuJu, and she was the one person who understood me inside and out besides my bestie Keshia. I truly believe that if it wasn't for her I don't think I would have graduated high school.

High school was nothing big. I graduated from Franklin High School, which people called a "fashion show." Every day people would look extra nice, you know, with the new Jordans and all.

It was okay, nothing too serious, but I also did not care. I did have a boyfriend in high school, but he had already graduated, and it was more like puppy love now that I look back at it. I can say though that I was head over heels at the time because that was my first experience of what I thought was love. I used to get picked up in his car (it was a 1985 Lincoln) thinking, "Yea, he got a car." I couldn't stop talking to him on the phone or texting. I mean, I was sixteen at the time.

Even though it was my first serious relationship, it was also my first heartbreak. When I tell you I thought I was so in love, I mean no one could tell me nothing. I was going through so many emotions I just did not know what to do.

Years later, I realized that I was never taught how to handle my emotions or what to do if I was sad. I had learned to shut down and push the issue away when I got mad, and that was a problem.

Chapter 3

LOVING SOMEONE IS EASY BUT LETTING GO IS SOMETHING ELSE

Now is the part where I talk about my daughter's father. I was young and thought I knew it all. I was out of control, but I was also slowly getting my act together. I went on a trip with my sister and friend to dirty south Atlanta, Georgia. When I tell you that it was an interesting trip, it sure was.

We had decided to take a Greyhound bus to Atlanta, don't even ask me why. I was only eighteen years old at the time, so I just went with the flow. That was probably the longest ride ever. I believe it was four days, and it had so many damn stops.

We made one of those stops in the middle of nowhere. It was more of a restroom stop, but new people got on the bus, too. I noticed this tall man. He had all black on, which was weird because we were in eighty-five-degree weather. However, he had a smile that could make you weak.

He had a country accent, and he asked, "Can I get by you?" I was so in shock. He was just so FINE! My teenage hormones were kicking in, and when we started to talk on the bus ride, I could not stop laughing with everything he said.

He told me his stop was is in Missouri and that he was from there. That twenty-four hours we talked about almost everything. I was having an experience with someone that I was truly interested in. When we stopped in St. Louis, we said our good byes and we never saw each other again.

For the rest of the bus ride, the driver was so loud that I knew no matter what, we were going to get to Atlanta on time. We arrived late at night, and I remember seeing all black people, which was great! The energy was everything. We got picked up by my friend's grandparents, who are the most beautiful people on the planet. We arrived at their home in College Park off Savoy Street, where the homes are beautiful too.

The next morning, I woke up to the smell of some good food. Breakfast was everything and Grandma was already starting lunch. It was just perfect. We had our day planned, but we did go and walk around the neighborhood. We also had to pick up her little cousin at a friend's house. As we walked by the side of the road, I noticed there were no sidewalks. We started looking at the homes, owned by lawyers, retired professors, and businesspeople. I could hear kids in the yards and watched them play in front of the houses. Seeing black families was everything. I started to hear music. We were getting closer to where we were picking up her cousin, and the music started to get closer, too. Then here came this all-white truck speeding down the street.

I jumped onto the grass and almost tripped over my own foot. The car made a hard stop and reversed backwards. The driver's window started to lower, and a deep Southern voice said, "You good?" I started to wipe any dirt off my clothes and replied, "Do you know how to drive? You almost hit me!"

That Southern voice grabbed my attention like no other. He started to apologize for driving recklessly. He had his friend on the passenger side, and the friend asked me if I wanted to hang out, but I wasn't even paying attention to him. All eyes were on the driver. He was wearing a white shirt and had his hat to the side. For some reason I was drawn to him. He asked me, "Where you from?" and I told him "Washington." He assumed D.C., and I laughed and said, "No, Seattle, Washington," and of course he said, "Where it rain all the time?" He had a sense of humor and he was smooth with it. He asked for my number and wanted to take me out. I explained to him that I was with family that day, but he was determined and insisted that we all come.

Later that night he took us to Cascade Skating, and yes, it was just like the movie *ATL*. We had a good time even though I did not know what I was doing. Later that evening we talked on the phone, and he wanted to take me out again. I told him that I was staying with my friend's grandparents, and he came to the door the next night to ask permission to take me out.

We drove all over Atlanta and had dinner at a Mexican restaurant. I knew (well, at the time, ladies) I wanted to be with him forever. He dropped me off, and I was sad because I knew I would be leaving. I was such a dumbass.

I got back to Seattle and all I could do was think about him. High school was over and I was now headed to college. We had a graduation party and my eighteenth birthday party combined, and I would go upstairs and text him or call him throughout the party. I knew I was leaving for Atlanta. My family was not happy about it, but sure enough, I left for Atlanta in August. We set me up with a place, school, and work.

However, the rain followed me from Seattle. It was nice for a while, but then the abuse started. I think that emotional abuse is worse than physical because you can at least attempt to hide the bruises of physical abuse, but I experienced both. Within just a few months, I was cheated on, hit, and verbally abused. It got physical, and I knew I had to leave.

There was a lady that lived in the same hallway as me. She was about forty years old, single, and had an older son. She saw me outside once by the door. She approached me and said, "If you need a phone or need to leave, come to my door." I did not realize at the time that was a sign.

One night he was acting weird. I asked him what was wrong, and he broke down, telling me, "I slept with someone else." He tried to comfort me, but I would not listen, and then he started to get aggressive. I had never been hit before by someone I was in a relationship with. Later that night I decided to leave. I had some friends I had met in Atlanta. I called one up and she came and got me. I went over to her home and I was crying so hard I felt that I couldn't breathe.

The next morning, I woke up with tears and a headache. I looked at my phone and I had missed calls from him. I finally called him and told him I was leaving and I would grab my things. A few hours later my friend, her boyfriend, and his brother came with me to grab my things. It was the hardest experience I had ever had to go through. He then walked in and started to yell, but this time I was not going to let him hit me. He got into my face and started to push me, and I pushed back with all I had. He gave me a look of evil. I grabbed what I could, and seven hours later I was at the airport heading back to Seattle with a plus one.

Love, Sex, and Sorrow

Chapter 4

FACE TO FACE

I finally landed back home and felt nervous and full of anxiety coming down the escalator and seeing my mom and sisters waiting for me. I felt welcomed, but I knew my childhood issues would stir up soon.

Remember that my parents split up when I was twelve years old. I wanted to live with my dad because my mother and I did not see eye to eye. I think she knew that, and so I left and lived with my dad until I graduated high school. My dad did have his flaws, but I could tell that they were from hurt. When I was about fifteen years old, my dad remarried. My stepmother had three older children, and our family was kind of like the Brady Bunch. It was an adjustment, but I had never had an older sister, so that was nice even though I knew I could be a bad influence. We would go out and kick it. I would even use her ID when she turned eighteen so I can go to the club. I was such a hurt teenager. My dad had another child so that made us a total of eight kids on both sides. It was hard at first, but now that we are adults it is so fun when we get together.

Now my mother and I had become estranged, so when I came from Atlanta, I felt that I did not know her. I did not feel any connection, but I knew I had to tell her that I was pregnant. I was eighteen years old, and I did not know what to do. I could keep it hidden only for a little while. I mean, I am only four foot eleven, and I felt that my pregnancy was moving fast.

I gave birth in July. I told myself I would never have another child and go through that pain again (I spoke too soon).

After coming from the hospital, I was so nervous with my child. I had never held a baby before or even changed a diaper. All my aunts would take turns to come over and check on me while my mother was at work.

I knew I had to start having confidence in myself. I enrolled in classes and picked up a part-time job at Home Depot. I was a cashier and did learn a lot. We would have all types of people coming in and some of the contractors were cute. On the other hand, we had plenty of people stealing. I ended up making some friends there, and it was pretty cool.

One particular friend was about six feet tall. We will call him "white boy." Now white boy was from West Seattle, he had some swang. He was such a gentleman. We would always go outside and just talk. He worked as a loader, helping people put the heavy items into their car. Now I had never looked at a white boy before, but he was different. We would talk for hours. A few months went past and we would hang out at work, until one day he asked me on a date. That was the first time a man ever asked me properly. I did tell him I would have to get back to him because I had a child. A week later, he took me out. We started to talk about our families, and that was the first time I realized that yea, he was white, but he went through some similar shit. He was raised by his single mother (though she did have a boyfriend) and his grandmother. He then took me home and did something I had never experienced before. This guy opened my door and actually walked me to my front door.

I stopped him at the gate, saying, "What the fuck are you doing?"

He said, "I am walking you to the door."

"Why?"

"That is what a man is supposed to do when taking a woman out."

I knew then I was in some shit.

The next day he asked to hang out again. We went out to eat and had some fun. I told him that I had bought a car, and he was happy for me, but then I had to tell him I did not have a legal license.

You see, I had taken a driver's education class and gotten my permit. I was not the best though, and I had even crashed my brother's car, not to mention hit a parked car once as well. I knew I should not be on the road, but he told me, "Don't worry, I got you." Lord behold, white boy taught me how to drive, and I got my license. The summer creeped up on us, and I was turning twenty-one years old. White boy's mom was getting married and I was invited to her wedding in Hawaii, so I asked my older sister if she wanted to come. The wedding was so nice. White people actually go somewhere for their wedding and it's big, but now a traditional African wedding is a whole damn event.

The only people you would know is your wedding party.

We flew back to Seattle and me and white boy was cool but I started to drift away. I felt that he was too clingy at the time. Now I wish I could take that back, and wish I had someone who was just like that. But a few weeks passed and we ended our relationship. I knew I was not right for him. I can look back now and realize he was someone special, that I pretty much grew up with him.

Love, Sex, and Sorrow

Chapter 5

ALWAYS BE CAREFUL HOW
YOU MEET SOMEONE

I started to get serious about school. I was involved in many different groups and met some interesting people there. I got a work-study job with the diversity center. It was not called that, but let's just say we had a good group of people that are friends even today. We had a boss that every student in that school was obsessed with. He worked a lot, especially with people of color. I, on the other hand, never looked at him in any way but like a brother. He had a beautiful smile and was soft spoken. He was the ideal black male that many women like. A few months passed and my boss introduced us to his friend who had gotten a job at the college. He was goofy but interesting at the same time. We did not have a big age gap, and when he would pop up at the center we would make small talk. He would ask me questions about myself and I asked him questions, too. He would always be joking around. One day I was closing the center and he was in the lobby. He asked me what plans I had for the evening, and I told him I was going home. He asked for my number and I didn't think anything of it at the time. A few weeks later, he asked if we could hang out alone.

I did not know what to expect when we linked up for the first time. We talked about relationships and he talked about how he had been in a long-term one for a while. Every time he spoke her name I could tell he was in pain. When we got back to his car, he leaned over and kissed me. Now I had not kissed a man in a long time, not since white boy. He said he had a good time and we would see each other again.

Now going to my classes and seeing him was so awkward, and he would send me text messages and speak to me by my car. We started meeting up with each other in secret, but I knew he told my boss because they were friends. After a while I knew I was catching feelings, but I did not want to tell him. One night he told me how he thought we should stop because he was thinking about getting back with his ex-girlfriend. I knew what she meant to him, so I did understand, but damn! At this point in my life I really did not understand dating or even having someone as a secret. Now that I am in my thirties, I know the difference. We said our good byes, and when we saw each other later it was pure friendship and lots of smiles.

Chapter 6
ROAD TRIP

I was in the last year of completing my associate's degree. It had been two years of academic dedication and different men, never knowing the two would go hand in hand. My older sister was going to college at Washington State University, about five hours away. This particular weekend, my friends and I were going to drive there and have what they called a "moms' weekend." We took my friend's car and I had my home girl Angel with me. She is the dopest girl and she is always there for me. We hopped in the car, took the blunt out, and started to smoke.

We ended up getting a little lost in Walla Walla, but I got hold of my sister and she directed us back to the main road. We arrived pretty late, like ten pm, but we knew it was time to kick it. My sister made lasagna and we had bottles. I loved me some circo. We went to a bar and got wasted, and we were dancing and having fun.

The next day we made the short drive to Idaho. We went to Macy's because they were having a crazy shoe sale, and the line wrapped around the corner. When we got there, I grabbed my sister and friend and somehow got us in the front of the line. It was crazy. People were grabbing all types of shoes and bags. I was going through the boots and my sister came across some Coach shoes that we got for thirty bucks. We came out with at least three boxes of shoes that we thought were

cute. Now we started to get ready for the night.

Chapter 7

SMOKE AND MIRRORS

The second night in Pullman we went to the mutual culture night. This show happens every year at different colleges around Washington. Everyone from Seattle comes down to represent their culture or perform, then everyone goes to all types of parties like sorority parties and of course the African party. We enjoyed the show and seeing people we knew doing our culture's dance. I even saw one of my older brothers who came with his friends, too. We all head to the after party, and we were loving it. I saw my god sister who at the time was going to Eastern Washington

University, not far at all. She was with some friends, but I got into a fight with one of them. My god sister did not know anything about this. I guess her friend did not tell her how it all went down on Othello Park. The girl didn't say much, but I was ready. I do look back and wish we squashed some childhood beef, because the girl is dead now. She was found murdered. It was sad how she left this earth.

We started to dance and the guys there were pretty cool but nothing major. The night was young and we went to a house party. It was pretty packed. Music was going, people were dancing, smoking, and drinking. I stayed in the hallway while my sister talked to her friend. My home girl Angel was talking to some guy, too. You see, I might come off like I can talk to anyone, but at that time, I knew I was going through something internally. I never talked about it or even spoke to myself about it.

The music was getting louder and more people started to dance. I moved myself against the wall. The music started to get more sexual. More people were slow dancing. The music in the background was playing Jodeci's "Feenin'." The lights were turned down and it was on. I was still against this wall trying to figure out how the hell I going to see.

All of a sudden, the music stopped and there was a problem with the electricity. Now it was pitch black and I did get a little scared because I couldn't see anything. I started to slide sideways against the wall. That is when I touched a hand, and a voice nearby told me, "Don't be scared." The lights turned on. He was standing right next to me, and he asked me if I was okay since I did bump into him. His eyes were deep brown and he had long lashes. He was wearing a baseball cap and jacket. I replied, "Yea, sorry." He walked away after a friend that was calling his name, and I told myself that I was going to marry this guy. We started to leave the party to head to the next one, and on our way out he said, "Glad you are okay." We went to the next party and got back to the house late.

The next day we packed up and hit the road, but I couldn't stop thinking about this guy. I wished I could have at least known his name.

Chapter 8

BE CAREFUL WHAT
YOU WISH FOR,
GOD ALWAYS HAS A REASON

After we came back from my sister's school, I could not stop thinking about this guy. Every weekend there was another college culture event, and we decided to go to another one the following weekend. We went to the University of Washington, and it was packed. We got to the show, and it was nice seeing all the dances.

Later that day we headed to an after party, which was another packed party with all the same people I knew. I saw my older cousins, old friends. Right across from the bathroom I saw the guy from the weekend before. I knew I couldn't just go up to him because I did not want to seem thirsty. My homegirl whispered in my ear, "Oh shit girl, isn't that the dude from WSU?" I felt numb, so she dragged me to the dance floor. We were dancing and laughing until I felt someone behind me. I felt the heat and his hand grabbed my wrist. He pulled me closer and started to dance with me. I felt so weak, but he was so soft. We started to walk away from the dance floor, somewhere a little quieter. He asked me my name and who I was with. He was so soft spoken. He told me that he was going to Western Washington University and invited my friends and me to their culture weekend. Before I could give him an answer, my homegirl answered for me. We laughed and parted ways.

The following weekend we drove up to Bellingham. Now I thought Seattle had a lot of white people, but damn! Bellingham really has a lot. We stopped at the grocery and the looks we were given were unbelievable. We had friends who were up there and going to school, so we linked up with one of them. We started to smoke and drink. We had arrived a day early before the performance so we could see the night life, and we heard about a club so we decided to head out. My homegirl asked me if my new friend had contacted me. I mean, he was the reason we were there. I went to the bar and saw him. He walked up to me and offered to buy me a drink, but we could barely talk because it was so loud. We ended the night with a hug and he told me he would see me at the event.

The next day we saw another show and went to another after party, but it was different and we could talk this time. I started to ask him more questions. He was from Seattle, but the north side. He asked me if we could go on a date when he drove back home for the summer. I accepted, and the sorrow began. I just didn't know it yet.

Chapter 9
SUMMER NIGHTS

Summer in Seattle is the most beautiful time. Plus, my birthday is in summer. All the beaches, BBQ, and long summer nights. He finally came back home, and our first date was at Green Lake. It was so nice. When the sun is out in Seattle, everyone is out too, and no one is home. We started walking around the neighborhood, and he took me to a taco spot. Tacos are one of my favorite things to eat, besides some mac and cheese. We spoke about our families and where we grew up. We also talked about who we knew, and we had a common friend. You see, his homeboy was dating my best friend's sister (of course, I called my best friend later that evening to ask her questions). The conversation with him started to get deep. I told him I do have a child, and he said it didn't bother him. That felt like a breath of fresh air. There was something about him I could not figure out, and I wanted to know more. Later that night I went home, and we spoke for hours over the phone.

We were together every day after work. He came with me out to the clubs and we were enjoying ourselves. I even met his siblings and he met mine.

Fall quarter started. He went back to school, but we arranged for time to see each other. One weekend I brought my homegirl Princess. Now Princess is so dope and gorgeous. However, don't ever cross her. She always and until this day is my favorite person. We're always laughing. When we arrived, he started to cook and laugh with the guys. Dating in college, especially long-distance dating, is hard. You will find out who they really are. The same night we were taking shots and we headed to the club. After the club I saw a family friend and I was in his car waiting for my friend. My girl Princess grabbed me and said, "Isn't that your dude talking to some girl?" I started to walk up and I heard him telling this young lady that she needs to go away. She started to yell and push him. My home girl Princess ran up so fast, I had to stop her. The girl was grabbed by her friend and started to cry. I had started back towards the car and he was running to me. I was so upset. How could he try and play me in front of my face? Meanwhile, my homegirl was ready to fight, so I was trying to calm her down. We got into the car and we sat in silence. We went back to his place and I was still silent. He started to explain himself. You know, the same bullshit: "It was nothing, all she did was give me some head, she is nothing." All I heard was blah, blah, blah. I told him it's over and we should stop talking. He continued to explain and he said he could prove to me that he was not playing me.

The next day, we spoke and I could see that he was serious. I was going to give him another chance.

Chapter 10

WHEN SOMEONE SHOWS YOU WHO THEY ARE THE FIRST TIME, BELIEVE IT

Our relationship started to get serious, and we celebrated birthdays and went to events together. We even started going camping with our friends. My best friend and her sister knew him, and I gained some friends as well. We had a date planned, but he said he wanted to stop somewhere first. We ended up at his house, and when we got to the door, he told me that he wanted me to meet his parents. Now let me give you a little background. When African parents are going to meet someone that you are dating, some of them automatically think you are getting married. I started to walk back to the car because I knew this could not happen. He pretty much dragged me inside to meet his mother. She was in the living room with her brother and they were drinking coffee. I couldn't even speak. She said hi and asked how I was. We stayed about ten minutes and left. During the car ride, I didn't really say much, but my gut was telling me that something was not right.

The next day he came to my work and I finally told him that I thought his mom didn't like me and I wasn't sure why he had brought me over. He said, "She is like that, don't worry." He told me he wanted me to get a dress for the coming Saturday night and that he wanted to tell me something then. I agreed, but I knew I had to end this relationship.

He picked me up and we went to dinner. We went to Bellevue, and it was so nice and romantic. He started to tell me that he was enjoying our time together. I was thinking, "Shit, I wanted to end the relationship before he does this." Then he says, "I love you." I was numb and did not say a word for about a minute. I was thinking, "Do I know what love is? Do I love him or do I love the idea that I can actually be a family?" But I came out with, "I love you, too." My stomach was turning. I guess god gives you signs that you can miss.

A week later we met up and he pulled out a box. He asked me to marry him, and I accepted. There was no romantic proposal, and I knew this relationship would be a challenge. I knew it was not right, but I was thinking with my heart and not my mind. I've learned now that you have to be smart when picking someone and sometimes the heart gets in the way.

That Saturday we went out and a few friends joined us while we were celebrating. Even though we were happy, I knew our families would have something to say. You see, in our culture, the man is supposed to go with the elders to the woman's house and ask her father. Now, that was the plan. However, they stood him up. My family was supportive, but I knew what they were doing for me. Weeks passed and I could tell he was hurting. We went to his mother's house to talk about our engagement. It was his mom and me face to face. She offered me some coffee, and while she was pouring she asked her son to grab something for her in her bedroom. When he went, she looked at me and said, "You are a good person. I know you are a single mom and going to school, but my son is not a husband yet. You guys should take your time." I tried to explain to her that he was good and we could handle this. She told me how the family does not agree. I understood her but I could not say anything. We left and I tried to explain to him that maybe we should wait. He insisted that no, they would agree with this. I knew our engagement was going to be a mess and I felt that our relationship probably would not work out.

Love, Sex, and Sorrow

Chapter 11

I GUESS I AM
SUPPOSED TO BE HAPPY

We set our engagement party for the month of June. Yea, it seems stupid to do one, but we were young. I was twenty-three years old. Everyone knew about this engagement party, and my family was cooking for weeks. My friends and I went to look at some dresses and were getting everything together. Things between my fiancé and me were okay, but I knew he was hurt inside. The day of the party came and everyone showed up except for his parents. We had a good time, and people were drinking and eating. The night was incredible, and everything was good for a moment.

A few months after that is when reality kicked in. He was trying to find another job, and we were moving into our new place across the street from my mom's house. I could tell things were not going well. We would argue more than ever and he would get aggressive with me.

He finally got a security job at Amazon, which was nice because he would work nights and we would hang out during the day. I also had classes, so we were busy. We were finally on good terms. We would smoke and drink and go out with our friends, or we would take my daughter out and just be a family.

One day I started to feel a little off, but I knew I had a doctor's appointment soon. I knew I had to grab myself another pack of birth controls pills, and I went into the appointment like any other every three months, just like the doctor wanted me to. She asked how was I doing. I told her I had been feeling a little off, but I thought it was just because I completed my three months of birth control. She said, "Okay, let's check." I went to the bathroom and the doctor came back in the room and told me she was unable to renew my birth control. She said, "You're pregnant, but I have some concerns." She did an ultrasound and there was no heartbeat. I told her that I had seen some blood the other day, but I had just thought it was my period because it was not much. She asked me if I had been feeling a little weak. I told her that yes, I had. She got a second opinion and confirmed that I was having a miscarriage. I had never experienced that before. I started to blame myself, like how could I not know? She said I was only about six weeks along. I started telling the doctor that I had been drinking—was that the cause? She said that it could have been or it could always be not the right time. She explained what my body would be going through next. I went to my car and called him. I told him we needed to talk. I went home, and I just said to him, "I am in the middle of a miscarriage." He was sympathetic and asked if I was okay.

You see, I did feel bad, but something came over me and told me that this was supposed to happen and that it would be okay. I guess everyone has that intuition. For the next couple of weeks, I was quiet. I didn't know what to do or even how to act. I was lost in my own body.

Chapter 12
JUST BREATH

We had been together about three years, and I knew we were not the same. He started to act and think differently. He would be gone long random hours, and we would continue to fight. August was the rough month. We decided to split up, and I started a new job close to the airport. I worked as a cashier at a shuttle service. It was twelve days before my twenty-fifth birthday, and I was trying to figure where me and my girls were going in Belltown and what I was going to wear. I got off work and grabbed a table. We had a good time, but I knew my relationship was over. At this time we were not talking. You see, two weeks before, we were in the car and he told me he wanted to end the relationship. He knew his family was not happy. I was just trying to be there. We argued and I said, "Fuck it, then." He packed his shit and it was done. We still had our phones under each other's names, and we had about a month left. Then we would end the contract.

The weekend of my birthday, he reached out and gave me some money as a birthday gift. I was angry. How can he just drop off money and that's it? He was trying to contact me, but I was ignoring his call until we had to meet up to end this phone contract.

One day in September, I was at work and my phone was going off. It was some type of alarm, but I had never seen this before on my phone. I kept seeing my little sister's name, like she lost her phone. So, being not all the way there, I called her and she picked up. I asked her if she was on her phone, and she said, "Sis, how else am I talking to you?" I literally was lost.

It was time for me to leave work, and my phone was still going off. I started to drive to get my daughter from daycare, and I turned left onto the back street. I saw a black SUV behind me that was driving kind of close, but I didn't think anything about it. The next minute this car was beside me, and the passenger window rolled down. Now this road is a two-way street, so he was driving the wrong way. I saw a guy and bullets started to hit my car. I screamed. I was in my body but I wasn't, if you know what I mean. I sped up and hit the corner. I thought I had lost him, but nope, he pulled up and started shooting the driver's side. I hopped over to the passenger side and climbed out the door. I left everything and started to run. He jumped out of his car and it started to roll back into someone's yard. He was right before my eyes and we were face to face. He pushed me against the fence and shot me on the side. I fell to the ground. Then he picked me up and pointed the gun to my head. The gun would not go off. It was stuck. I tried to get myself up but kept falling. He finally got the gun to shoot, but the bullets missed. He went to reload and I heard someone in my ear, saying, "Get up and hit him now." I just replied and said, "I can't." I remember that while he was reloading, he asked me who I was talking to. I got up and punched him in the face. I would not stop. I ran for help, and I was shot again.

I was trying to find some help, and I saw a car pull over. It was my little sister on her way to pick up my mom. She jumped out of the car, and my attacker walked towards her. That is when I ran to her because he was walking with his gun. She called his name and he stopped and walked back to his car. I ended up on someone's doorsteps. I call her my angel. She opened the door and her eight-year-old grandson placed me on the couch with a blanket. Cops and an ambulance showed up. They put me in the ambulance. Everything was a blur, and I woke up with lights and white coats all over me.

Made in the USA
Columbia, SC
02 August 2022

63856017R00035